A. M. Anderson Sr.

For Broke AZZ People

Volume 1

How to Buy
A Home

Written By:
A. M. Anderson Sr.

For Broke AZZ People - Volume 1 - How to Buy A Home

ISBN-13: 978-0615861340
ISBN-10: 0615861340

Written By: A. M. Anderson Sr.

Published By:
Anderson Inc.
P.O. Box 37881
Jacksonville, FL 32236

The publication is designed to provide accurate and authoritative information in regard to the subject matter covered. It is sold with the understanding the publisher is not engaged in rendering legal, accounting, or other professional services. If legal advice or other expert assistance is required, the services of a competent professional person should be sought.

Anderson Inc. Publishing Books are available at special discounts for bulk purchases, sales promotions, fundraisers, or educational purposes.

Email: andersoninc@netzero.com

A. M. Anderson Sr.

A. M. Anderson Sr.

CONTENTS

CHAPTER 1

The Definition of Poor and Broke

WAIT! First of all let's get one thing straight – there is a difference between POOR and BROKE.

<u>**Poor** is a condition,</u> like living in a 3rd world country; having no money or possessions; not having enough money for the basic things that people need to live properly and no way of getting those things.

▪ *We are too poor to buy anything.*

<u>**Broke** is temporary,</u> like not having any money at this time; to spend or lose all of your money.

▪ *Can I borrow 10 dollars? I'm broke until payday.*

▪ *He went broke after spending his whole paycheck.*

If you will receive income next week when you get paid or on the 1st of the month when your disability or social security check comes or at the 1st of the year when you get an income tax refund you are not poor, you are just broke at the time. It's what you do with your money that makes your AZZ broke.

Broke is a state of mind, your mind. One may say having no money is poor, I say "NOT"!

As long as you appreciate your inner blessings, you can turn it into income and you will never be poor. Hey, that sounds like a book! Ok it is a book. Guess whose book? Yes, my book.

Appreciate Your Inner Blessings And Turn It Into Income

A great book to have and you can find it at:
www.TodayBiz.info
Go get your blessing!!!!

It's never ok to be poor but in my opinion these days it is common to be broke.

Whether you have money or you are broke shouldn't determine your happiness. Your happiness should come from the heart, not the wallet, even though I know a few women that are happy with the size of my wallet.

Some people's opinion is you can't be broke and be happy at the same time. That's just some people's opinion.

You have to be willing to do whatever it takes

CHAPTER 2

The Definition of Broke AZZ People

My definition of broke AZZ people is as follows:

<u>**Broke,**</u> as mentioned in Chapter 1, is something temporary and related to your state of mind. If you live in the USA and don't have a job you can generate income by designing something, creating something or finding something to sell.

If someone is **broke** it's usually because they choose to be. Yes, one is broke because they choose to be.

Check this out: you come home from work and you are hungry. You say you are too tired to cook but you are hungry. You say you had a hard day at work and you are too tired to cook but you are hungry. You say the steaks are frozen and you had a hard day at work and are too tired to cook but you are hungry. You say you are not going to cook because the steaks are frozen and you had a hard day at work and you are too tired to cook but you are still hungry. Then you are hungry because you choose to be. The same way you are broke because you **choose** to be!

You have to be willing to do whatever it takes

Take the steaks out and let them thaw out. Kick off your shoes and relax. Read a book or watch the news as you wait for the steaks, maybe even take a soothing bath. Now you are no longer tired, you've forgotten about your hard day, the steaks are thawed out and you can go ahead and cook. The hunger problem is solved. In this case you need only eliminate the negatives to come to a positive conclusion.

Here's a good book to read:

The Formula: P / (U x K) + W = SUCCESS
specially chosen biblical scriptures to help you achieve success toward everything you do.

you can find it at
www.TodayBiz.info
Go get your blessing!!!!

You have to be willing to do whatever it takes.

In today's society broke usually comes from over spending not low earnings. We over spend because it's convenient to do so but few are looking at the cost of this convenience.

Check this out: for the convenience of a cell phone the cell phone company offers you a free phone with a two year contract and our broke AZZ's run and get one.

Is it really free when a two year contract adds up to about $100 a month? That's $2,400 over the two year contract. FREE phone? I think not!

I had my cell phone for seven or eight years and Sprint called me every month asking me to upgrade, offering me a free phone to do so. After the tenth time they called me I explained how I did not need to receive text messages or to have a camera on my phone. The salesmen said, "but Mr. Anderson, the phone is free." "Ok then Mr. Salesman give me the free phone and keep your two year contract," I replied. "No Mr. Anderson, it doesn't work like that," he said. "Well Mr. Salesman I don't need a $2,400 cell phone and you have a bless day."

That conversation was over 6 years ago and Sprint never called again to offer me a free phone. You have to be willing to do whatever it takes.

At that time I came up went the acronym AZZ.

AZZ is an acronym that stands for:

A: Ability   The ability to change the way you see things.

Z: Zap   Zap negative thoughts from your mind such as "I can't do."

Z: Zinger   This surprisingly simple piece of information that can change your future.

"AZZ"

You have to be willing to do whatever it takes

You have to be willing to do whatever it takes

CHAPTER 3

What Will It Take

You have to be willing to do whatever it takes.

1. Look at things differently
2. Get from under rent payments
3. Save money
4. Buy a home

Go from paying rent to owning your own home.

You give your church 10 % (tithes) right!

Uncle Sam takes out his percentage in taxes even before you receive yours.

You give what toward your new house? <u>0%</u>.

For every dollar you get, even if it's only one dollar, you should put a percentage aside toward your goal of buying your house. It is even possible to add the money you saved to your income tax refund and you can buy a cash house.

Yes, you can buy a house for **CASH!**

<u>NO RENT, NO MORTGAGE PAYMENTS!</u>

CHAPTER 4

Opinion versus Fact

This book is not my opinion on how to buy a house.

This book is not about how to get rich buying real estate.

This book is not about flipping houses.

This is not that type of book.

Look at the title - "For Broke AZZ People"

This book is about **how** I brought my 1st bank foreclosure house for CASH.

This book is about **why** I brought my 2nd cash house.

There is no need to give details on the 3rd cash house because then I would only be bragging on my blessings and this is not that type of book.

This book is based on what I actually did and that makes this information facts and not my opinion.

You have to be willing to do whatever it takes

CHAPTER 5

My Broke AZZ Paid CASH

You may ask, "what type of house can Broke AZZ people buy for cash?"

Answer:

Fixer-Upper Houses
And
Foreclosed Homes

You must be willing to roll up your sleeves and do the work.

A: Ability   The ability to change the way you see things.

Z: Zap   Zap negative thoughts from your mind such as "I can't do."

Z: Zinger   This surprisingly simple piece of information that can change your future.

CHAPTER 6

Definition of
Fixer-Upper Houses

A **fixer-upper** is a slang real estate word for a property that will require some repair work. Often they can be lived in while you work on it. They are popular with buyers who wish to raise the property's value to get a higher return on their investment, a practice known as flipping. It can also be a good **starter home for buyers on a budget.**

Home-improvement television shows touting do-it-yourself renovation techniques have made fixer-uppers more popular, but during a real estate downturn, with newer homes available at depressed prices, there is often reduced interest in this type of housing.

Inexperienced buyers frequently underestimate the amount and cost of repairs necessary to make a home livable or saleable. Structural and service issues such as a home's foundation or plumbing, which may not be visible at first, can require expensive, professional contracting work.

"You are looking for something **livable,** not saleable"

CHAPTER 7

Definition of
Foreclosed Homes

Foreclosed Homes present a situation in which a homeowner is unable to make principal and/or interest payments on his or her mortgage, so the lender, be it a bank or lending agency, can seize and sell the property as stipulated in the terms of the mortgage contract.

There's an old saying that suggests that opportunity is where you find it. **Note that it doesn't say "where it finds you."**

This old saying could easily be the mantra of the first time home buyer/investor. To such a home buyer, finding a great foreclosure property is like finding a diamond in the rough. With foreclosures always present in the real estate market, those "diamonds in the rough" are there for the taking by those that know what to look for. Because so few people are using foreclosure properties to create personal wealth, it leaves the playing field open for home buyers who are willing to roll up their sleeves, learn the skills and do the work.

You have to be willing to do whatever it takes

CHAPTER 8

How I Accomplished It

I'm Mr. Anderson Sr., aka Tony A. I'm here to explain to you ***how I brought my first foreclosed home for cash.***

My daughter and I was driving around different neighborhoods and we spotted this property with a big yard and a basketball court (my daughter loves to play basketball!) The house looked abandoned.

The photo was taken after I cut the grass

At the time my daughter, aka Princess Diva, was still recovering from a surgery that almost took her life a few months back. She mentioned how good it would be to have her own basketball court and the yard had plenty of room for all the trucks and trailers for my business.

Ok, the house was abandoned and I saw how happy my daughter would be to have her own basketball court.

I looked up the address at the City Property Appraiser's Office to locate the owner. It was bank owned and they gave me the contact info for the local real estate agent who was in charge of the property.

The realtor's name was Ms. Bonnie. She was a very informative and sweet middle aged lady. She met my daughter and I at the house where I asked a lot of questions which she patiently answered.

Ms. Bonnie was the owner of a real estate agency and she asked me if she could look up more houses for me because she knew she could find houses in better condition than this one. I asked her if they would have a basketball court, a yard as big as this one at around the same asking price. She looked me right in the eyes, smiled and said "Mr. Anderson I really don't think so".

My next step was to make an offer, the asking price was $17,000 but the house had nothing inside of it.

Ms. Bonnie informed me that the bank was only taking cash offers on this house and the house has been on the market for 788 days. That was good for me because the longer a house is on the market the more it cost the bank, so the bank really wants to get rid of it.

The bank was asking $17,000 for the house. The land was valued at $7,000. I was going to offer the Bank $10,000 for the house.

But WAIT! If you look at the front of the house, you can see that there is a demolition sticker from the City posted next to the front door.

My language changed from "house" to "property"

Ok now please note, I'm not buying a house, I'm buying the land. My offer now is $6,000 for the **property**.

You have to be willing to do whatever it takes

Ms. Bonnie asked "is that your final offer?" I looked her right in the eyes, smiled and said, "I'm broke so YES!

It usually takes from 7 to 10 business days for the bank to respond. Three days later Ms. Bonnie called me and said the bank had accepted our offer and within three weeks we signed the documents and took possession of the house, I mean the property.

My daughter and I at closing.

You have to be willing to do whatever it takes

Front of house – before fixing up

Front of House – after a little fix-up

You have to be willing to do whatever it takes

Living Room - before

Living Room – after a little fixing-up

You have to be willing to do whatever it takes

Bath Room – before

Bath Room – after a little fixing-up

You have to be willing to do whatever it takes

Kitchen - before

Kitchen – half way – with raised floor in cooking area

You have to be willing to do whatever it takes

Kitchen – double sink

Kitchen – flat surface stove top

You have to be willing to do whatever it takes

You have to be willing to do whatever it takes

Now let me explain *why I brought my second cash home.*

My daughter was in the 10th grade when her medical problems started. After her surgery she was home schooled. Now she wanted to go back to school to complete the 12th grade and participate in the high school prom. She was disappointed when no one asked her to go to the prom.

The first problem was she looked 13 years old and the second problem was she was new at school and everyone thought she was a freshman. With no date for the prom she decided to go with her best friend.

The month of May is a very good month, not because my birthday is in that month but because my baby girl was graduating and her birthday is in that month. I had to think of something big to get her because she been through a lot the last two years and had also experienced a lot of disappointment.

I thought about how much fun she had helping me renovate the first house I brought, especially the memories of us playing basketball when we took our breaks while fixing up the house.

Something big, I thought! What's bigger than a house! I could buy my baby girl a cash house and we could work on it together.

So I went looking for a cash house, this time one that required less work.

I was looking for four things in the house.

1. An existing electric meter
2. A roof in good condition with no leaks
3. No liens on the property
4. Low back taxes if any are due

The house I found was from a private owner. The air conditioning unit was stolen along with the hot water heater and the kitchen sink. No really, the kitchen sink was gone.

The house had a hole in the kitchen ceiling and a hole in the utility room ceiling.

I negotiated with the owner on a price. I asked him to carry the note for five years. He said he would reduce the price if I paid it off in two years. I asked if he would reduce it even more if I paid cash. He agreed and within 30 days my baby girl had her first cash house at the age of 18.

I brought the house for my daughter so she could have rental property and bank the rent money she collected. Instead she decided to move in it and live rent free.

House – front view

House – back view

You have to be willing to do whatever it takes

Kitchen - hole in ceiling

Kitchen - hole in ceiling repaired

You have to be willing to do whatever it takes

Kitchen – countertop without sink

Kitchen - countertop with double sink installed

You have to be willing to do whatever it takes

Free Fence to be installed by me

Digging holes for the fence

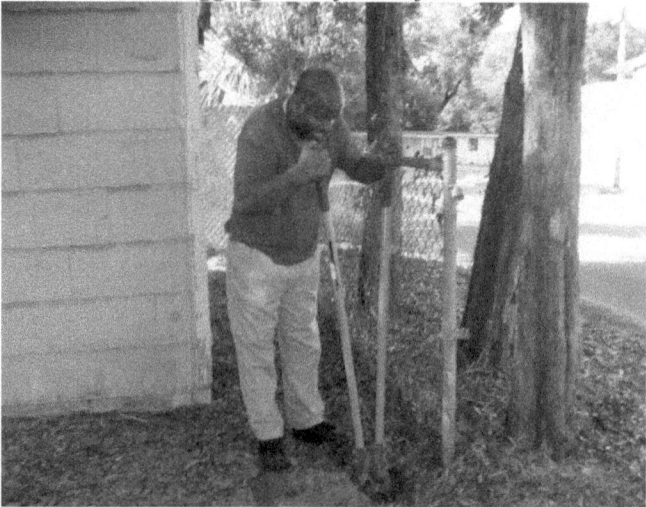

You have to be willing to do whatever it takes

Really, installing the fence myself

The fence installed

You have to be willing to do whatever it takes

House front without fence

House front with fence

You have to be willing to do whatever it takes

Back view without fence

Back view with fence

You have to be willing to do whatever it takes

CHAPTER 9

How You Can Do It

Buying a fixer-upper house or foreclosed home for the first time home buyer or first time investor can be a great investment.

One may ask, is it safe to buy a foreclosure? It's safe to buy a previously foreclosed house if title insurance is available on it.

You can find these properties on websites. Many of the websites will require a small fee. If you sign up on several sites the fees can add up.

Look at the title "For Broke AZZ People". So instead of going to the websites you should go riding around looking for vacant houses that have a posted sign or two in the window or on the door.

36
You have to be willing to do whatever it takes

One will say "In case of an emergency contact 1-800-number." Another note(s) may be from the city. Here's a little secret: the ones that have a note reading "In case of emergency" are usually bank owned properties.

Generally the banks are going to price the properties much lower than what the current market value is because they want to get rid of the properties as soon as they possibly can. It costs them money to carry these properties, so every month they keep them it's money out of their pocket.

When looking for property keep an eye out for properties that need only cosmetic improvements. Houses that could use new paint, carpeting or flooring are the least expensive and offer the fastest ability to move into or rent out. Larger problems such as bad roofs or faulty foundations are more expensive to fix.

Look for vacant homes that have not been kept up by the owner. These forgotten houses often have the most motivated seller you could hope to find.

When you find a property that you're interested in, contact a local real estate agent and ask them to look up the property to find the owner and the value of the property.

Once you've located the property that you're interested in, do your homework. Make sure there are no liens on the property. One can do this by hiring a title company or a lawyer who perform a title search on the property and make sure that it's clear and ready to be transferred to a new owner.

Look at the title "For Broke AZZ People". Dealing with bank foreclosures are a good thing because the banks works with local title companies that won't cost you anything.

Be particularly aggressive in negotiating with a bank. They're keen to sell a foreclosed home fast, as it's just sitting on their books doing nothing.

Ask your local real estate agent to submit the offer for you. It's going to be a much smoother process if you have someone representing you during this transaction just because banks like dealing with realtors and lawyers.

Understand that foreclosure means that because a home owner has become unable to pay the mortgage the lender has taken back the property. The legal steps involved will differ from state to state.

Tour the property and inspect it as closely as possible. Some foreclosures – unlike fixer-uppers – are in fairly good shape but often behind in maintenance. Usually the cheaper the property, the more work it will take.

Be prepared to perform an extensive search. Many fixer-uppers, particularly those in especially bad shape, don't command much attention, so you may have to hunt around. Drive through desirable neighborhoods to spot the right type of houses.

Buying a fixer-upper or bank foreclosure can be a profitable endeavor. There is a level of risk involved, not to mention a substantial commitment of time and effort on your part and long periods of time when you could be living in sawdust and paint odors.

You have to be willing to do whatever it takes.

Keep in mind that your ideal place to live may not be in your price range at the time. This is your starter home not your dream home.

Remember your house will be worth even more when your repairs are completed and this could be your first step toward your dream home.

Be patient. Unlike the folks on the Home and Garden television shows who make it look as though renovations happen within a few weekends, the right price fixer-uppers can take time to find and much longer to spruce up, particularly if you're holding down a day job and have minimum finances.

Advantages of a fixer-upper house

Fixer uppers can definitely be a great option for those with limited funding for their property purchase. Because fixer uppers are usually older, they often will be in well-established neighborhoods, with higher market values. Older homes will often have a lot of charm and desirable characteristics, such as bay windows, fireplaces and wooden floors. Once this type of property has been fixed up, the value can rise quickly and it becomes highly sought after.

Make whatever repairs and renovations are necessary and if possible move into your home as you are doing the work. You will live rent free and you will notice how much easier it will be to start saving money.

You have to be willing to do whatever it takes

CHAPTER 10

In Closing

You have to be willing to do whatever it takes.

**You must be willing to roll up your
sleeves and do the work.**

A: Ability The ability to change the way you see
things.
Z: Zap Zap negative thoughts from your
mind such as "I can't do."
Z: Zinger This surprisingly simple piece of
information that can change your future.

GOD BLESS!

The End

For Broke AZZ People - Volume 1 - How to Buy A Home

Written By:

A. M. Anderson Sr.

Published By:

Anderson Inc.
Publishing
P O Box 37881
Jacksonville, Fl. 32236
"We Publish Dreams"

For Broke AZZ People - Volume 1 - How to Buy A Home

A great book to have!

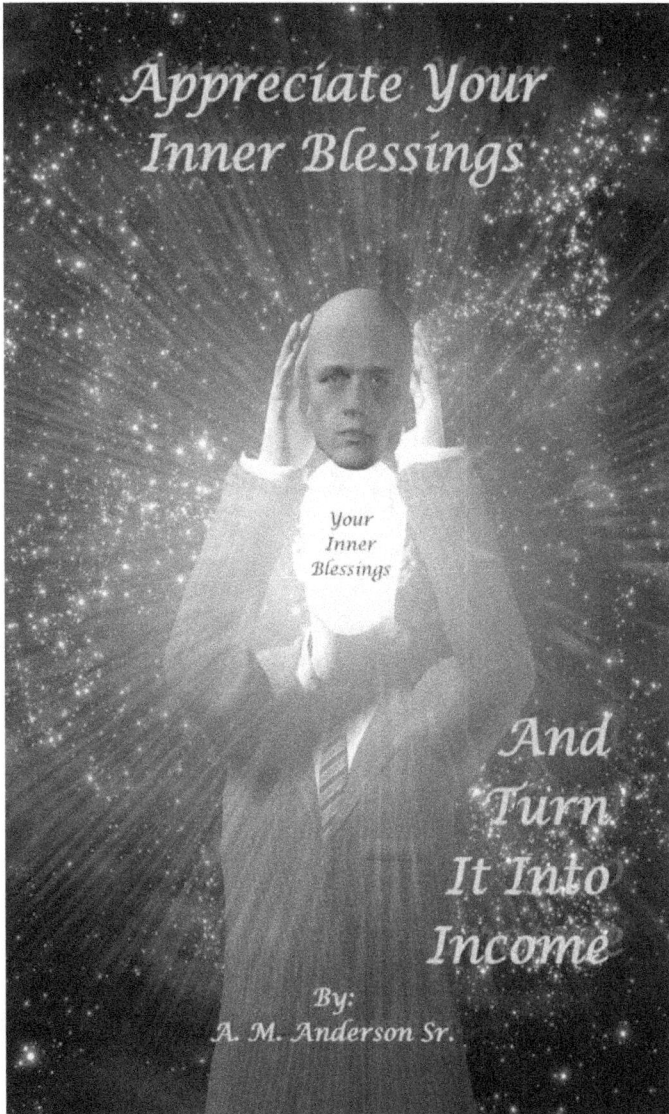

Appreciate Your
Inner Blessings

Your
Inner
Blessings

And
Turn
It Into
Income

By:
A. M. Anderson Sr.

Special Thanks To:

Anderson Games.

www.TodayBiz.info

Bring your family back to the dining room table with fun board games.

A family that plays together stays together.

Board games for the entire family.

The Corporate Ladder Game:

Corporate Ladder Board Game is fun, educational and entertaining. This game is a stepping stone into the world of business within the corporate structure. Corporate Ladder Game may help others change their lives from those that are easily manipulated ("followers") into those who are the go-getters ("leaders").

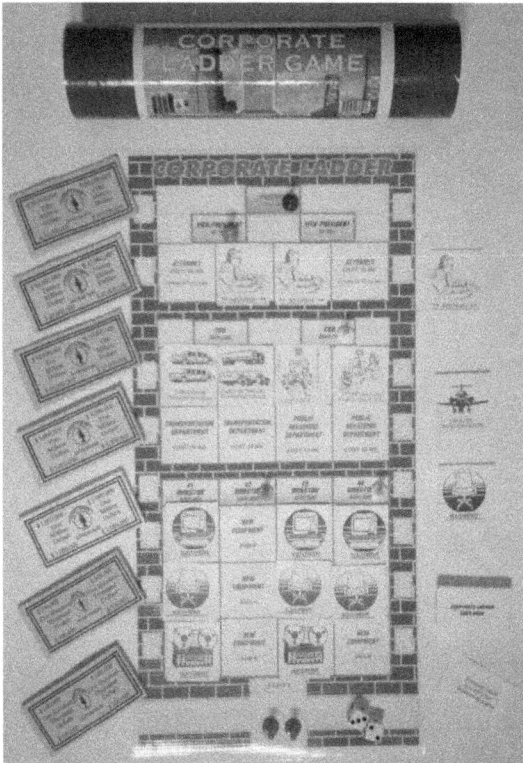

www.TodayBiz.info

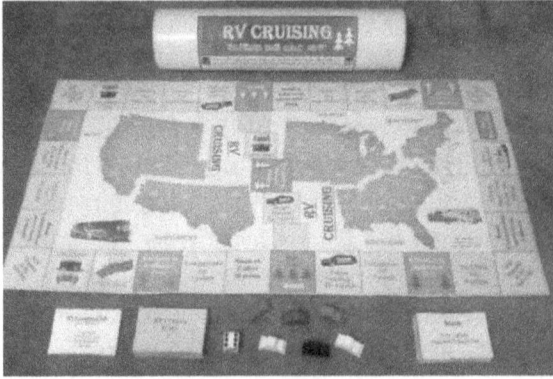

RV Cruising: Object of the Game: To travel around the country collecting as many National and State Park Cards as you can to earn points. The game is over at the end of the card deck. At the end of the game, the player with the most points wins the game.

Crime Alert Game: Object of the Game:
To collect as many tips as you can and turn them in so you can earn lots of money. At the end of the game, the player with the most money wins the game.

To order books
Go to www.TodayBiz.info
Or
Mail checks or money orders to:

Anderson Inc.
P.O. Box 37881
Jacksonville, FL 32236

Please send _____ copy (ies) of

For Broke AZZ People
Volume 1 - How to buy a Home

Name:_____

Address_____

City: _____ State: ___ Zip:_____

Telephone: (   ) _____ (   ) _____

Email: _____

I have enclosed $8.00 per book, S&H is
included for a total of $_____.

For bulk orders, wholesale rates or
appearances, you can reach us at
andersoninc@netzero.com or write to:

Anderson Inc. - P.O. Box 37881 - Jacksonville, FL 32236

For Broke AZZ People - Volume 1 - How to Buy A Home